# The Complete Guide to Search Engine Optimization for Starters and Beginners

# The Basics of SEO

## Anurag Kartik

**The Digital Version of this book is available at:**

https://www.amazon.com/dp/B01GT19AV8

**Content**

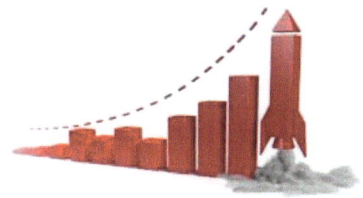

The Digital Version of This Book is available at:

## Chapter One: Prologue

SEO is both science and art. You need devotion and perseverance to rank your sites or your client's site.

Some top sites we have ranked are pepperfry.com for "Buy Furniture"; Bata.in for "Buy Shoes Online"; Makemytrip.com for "Buy Bus Tickets"; ebs.in for "Payment Gateway"; latestone.com for "Mobile Accessories".

No need to say that all these companies have millions of dollars in their bank account. I Provide SEO Consultancy to companies at $500 per project. If you want my help then contact at: shivshakti1949(at)outlook(dot)com.

Read the entire book and unleash traffic.


## Chapter 2: What are Search Engines?

Search Engines are nothing but glorified version of your windows explorer. They match the query you put in search box and give the most relevant results, sorted in an order. The first search engine was yahoo.com and in India –the first search engine was khoj.com. But after the advent of Google in 1999 – the other search engines took back seat, and Google slowly inched towards its dominant position. It has more than 63% market share and every day there are more than 1 Billion searches in Google. The other prominent search engines of our times are yahoo.com, bing.com, altavista.com, ask.com, seek.com, yandex.com and baidu.com.

The Alexa rank of Google.com is 1, of yahoo.com is 4, and of baidu.com is 6 and that of bing.com is 17. The President of Indian National Congress –Sonia Gandhi features as the most powerful women in India in all major search engines –at least there is something common in all search engines. I admire her and when she became my Internet friend –I asked what does she want to become in life? She replied to me: "I am a true patriot like my husband and fore-fathers; I want to serve my country till the last drop of blood. If Congress again comes in power then I want three portfolios –Home, Finance and External Affairs". I wished her all the best.

If you search Google then there are 189 Million search results about "Sonia Gandhi". Still Google gives the most relevant search results. It has more than 1 Million servers which keep on indexing 463,498,125,627,121,419 pages on internet.

## Chapter 3: How do Search Engines rank your Site?

Have you heard of Google Penguin; Google Panda or Google Humming Bird –they are nothing but algorithms developed by Google to rank your sites.

The sites are ranked on various factors. Let me elaborate these factors from Google's point of view:

- Domain Authority –The content in Wikipedia, LinkedIn and other top sites will have high ranking.
- Freshness of Content
- Number of do-follow backlinks
- Number of no-follow backlinks
- Social Signals from content posted in YouTube, Facebook, LinkedIn, SlideShare, Twitter etc.
- Keyword Density –The ideal keyword density in content should be 5-10%
- Meta Tags –So that Search Engines can crawl the keywords in Meta Tags.
- Relevance of Content

- No of Mentions in Social Media, Groups and Forums
- Page Rank – That is the quality of Backlinks
- Mobile Friendliness of Site –If your site is mobile friendly, ranking is higher.
- Age of the Site –Older the site, higher would be its ranking
- Popularity of the Site – Depending upon the Alexa Rank of Site, the keywords are ranked. (Suppose there are 1 million hits to your website within hour, and then all keywords would rank in top 10).
- Speed of the Site –The lesser time the site takes to load –higher it would be ranked.
- Security of the site –(https:// sites are ranked higher)

Now there is a graph which shows various factors for ranking of sites:

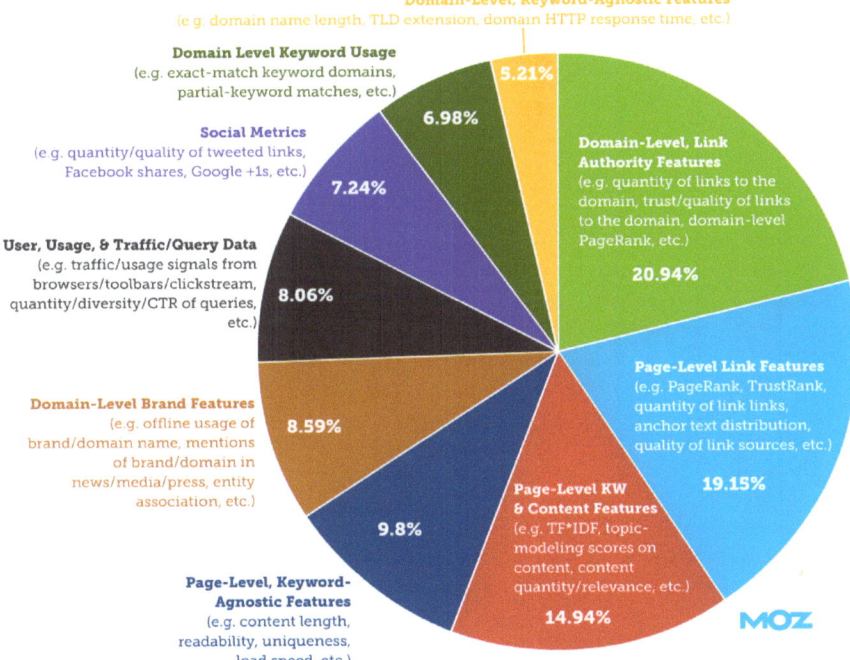

# Weighting of Thematic Clusters of Ranking Factors in Google
(based on survey responses by 128 SEO professionals in June 2013)

(Reproduced with permission from Moz)

## Chapter 4: The importance of Search Engine Rankings and Keyword Research

Now I elaborate the importance of Search Engine Ranking or Search Engine Optimization. Most companies need SEO. Below I have given the top 10 reasons elucidating that SEO is important:

- Online visibility improves conversions. Most of the people in India came to know about Flipkart, when they searched for a particular product and it was available on Flipkart.
- It generates leads. SEO is one of the best ways to generate leads. SEO is so great because it allows you to earn leads from a variety of different places and platforms online including YouTube, Flickr, Instagram and local search queries through Google, Bing, and Yahoo. In fact, SEO leads have a 29% close rate, while Social Media leads have 17%.
- You know about your competitors. When you search for a particular keyword, you would learn - who are your close competitors, and how you have to close ranks on them.
- SEO helps improve your visibility. By seeing your website, video, articles, posts and shares, people come to know about your products and would like to interact with you.
- SEO improves user experience of your site. By doing SEO your site has good navigation; website has relevant and unique content; website has no broken links or 404 errors. To get higher rankings you give your website an engaging design.
- SEO builds you brand reputation and credibility. By seeing your website in top of search results, people think that you are a good seminarian.
- It attracts the right people at the right time. Suppose someone is searching for old laptop, and your site surfaces at the top of results; then the visitor would be more interested to deal with you.
- It makes your site mobile friendly. To get good ranking, you have to make your website mobile friendly.
- SEO saves your advertising expense. SEO means free traffic for life. The money you might have spent on advertising is saved.
- SEO helps you to be a steady player. If there is constant flow of traffic to your website, even without generating much revenue, you would be steady with your biz.

There are a few factors which are taken in account when you want to rank a site with particular keywords:

Search Volume – The first factor is how many people are actually searching for a given keyword. The more people there are searching for a given keyword, the larger is the audience you can target. In contrast, if there is no one is searching for a given keyword, then there is no audience available to explore your content through search results.

Relevance – If your keywords are frequently searched in search engine, then it is great. But if it is not relevant to your business, then it would not yield revenues for you. Suppose your site is about removing alcohol addiction, and then it would be great if your site features in top searches for leave alcohol, and alcohol related diseases.

Competition —In any business there is competition, and so it is with SEO. There would be other sites with which you have to compete, and you have to rank well for given keywords to get good business. You should understand who are your potential customers, and what keywords will they search to get to you. If you match up with your competitors or beat them then you will definitely attract good traffic and get good revenue.

You should think about the solutions to the problems of your customers and come up with "Seed List" of Keywords, after that you should optimize your site for those keywords.

Now let us talk about content creation. You should create content that would be likely to be shared and promoted by others. You should create a content which solves your customer's problems. Reverse engineer what already works. Your content should be fail proof as much possible.

Share the information with others. Share your content tools and get great content from others. Get answers from experts in your niche and make your content compelling. When you recommend somebody, then it is likely that it adds as a value addition to your content too. You should focus on creating different contents, and then try to promote them through social media. You should be generous enough to highlight the people who have helped you with the content.

Now I will give you tips how to find the right keywords

1. Research the keywords —find the one which is right for you.
2. The keywords should have high search volume —many people should be looking for keywords.
3. The competition should be less for the given keyword.
4. The content of your site should support the keywords.

There are many tools which help you in finding the right keywords —but the most popular is Google's Search Based Keyword Tool. It provides result based on actual searches.

One of the strategies to attract traffic is to use the "The Long Tail" Keyword. Suppose you are selling pizza in Delhi; you can use cheesy-pizza-in-new-delhi as the page title and name and optimize for it.

## Chapter 5: Importance of Title and Meta Tags

I suppose you know the basic HTML, but for your convenience I am copying the lines of codes from my website:

```
<!DOCTYPE HTML>
<html>

<head>
  <title>Sunny -The Hot Religion,Shani Sanatan Dharam or Dharma. New
Religion Sunny, Venture Capital Funding, VC Funding Consultant, Work
```

```html
from Home, Work at Home, Online Jobs, Home Tutor, Online Tutor</title>
  <meta name="End of Kaliyuga,Hot Religion Sunny, Shani Sanatan Dharam
or Dharma, venture capital funding, vc funding, vc funding consultant,
work from home, work at home, online jobs, physics tutor, chemistry
tutor, maths tutor, biology tutor, home tutor delhi, home tutor mumbai,
home tutor chennai, home tutor bangalore, online tutoring, home tutor
uk, home tutor usa, home tutor canada, online tutoring, work from home,
freelance jobs, Shani Deva, New Religion, Sunny the Hot Religion,
Jihad, Islamic Fundamentalism, Hindu Extremism, Hindu Fundamentalist,
Religious Intolerance" content="End of Kaliyuga, Shani Deva, New
Religion, Sunny the Hot Religion, Jihad, Islamic Fundamentalism, Hindu
Extremism, Hindu Fundamentalist, Religious Intolerance" />
  <meta name="End of Kaliyuga,venture capital funding, vc funding, vc
funding consultant, work from home, work at home. online jobs, physics
tutor, chemistry tutor, maths tutor, biology tutor, home tutor delhi,
home tutor mumbai, home tutor chennai, home tutor bangalore, online
tutoring, home tutor uk, home tutor usa, home tutor canada, online
tutoring, work from home, freelance jobs, Shani Deva, New Religion,
Sunny the Hot Religion, Jihad, Islamic Fundamentalism, Hindu Extremism,
Hindu Fundamentalist, Religious Intolerance" content="End of Kaliyuga,
Shani Deva, New Religion, Sunny the Hot Religion, Jihad, Islamic
Fundamentalism, Hindu Extremism, Hindu Fundamentalist, Religious
Intolerance" />
  <meta http-equiv="content-type" content="text/html; charset=UTF-8" />
  <link rel="stylesheet" type="text/css" href="css/style.css" />
  <meta name="fl-verify" content="3048afb38b49ec8ae92213fb9a9964e7">
  <!-- modernizr enables HTML5 elements and feature detects -->
  <script type="text/javascript" src="js/modernizr-
1.5.min.js"></script>
</head>

<body>
```

If you note that the title, Meta tags come between the opening and closing <head> </head> tag. The appropriate title would help you to get indexed faster and higher rankings. The appropriate keywords in Meta Tags and description would help you higher rankings for the given keywords, and my strategy is to stuff as many keywords possible –as it is obvious from above. The text written in the Meta tag would be shown in the search result.

Descriptions in the Meta tags tell audiences what they can expect to find on your page, and they are persuaded those users to click. In a way, Meta descriptions are like Calls to Action.

These two images and the content above would give you a fair description of using Meta Tag.

**Chapter 6: Tags and Their Importance**

If you have been typing in MS Word, then you would be aware of Heading 1 <H1>, Heading 2 <H2> and Heading 3 <H3>. The best strategy to rank your site higher with the search engines would be to write all keywords in all three fonts <H1>, <H2>, <H3> maintaining a high keyword density.

As far as images are concerned then use the <alt> tag to name the images in your website with a keyword. This will help image to be indexed by search engines, and by image search also someone might reach your website.

Optimizing your codes

Search engines just do not read the text of your website, they also read the code of your website. So in the HTML code of your website, you should take care of these factors.

Title Tags

In the title tag, you should encase the title of your site.

For example:
<title> Sunny –The Hot Religion </title>
This title we have taken from our website www.igurucool.in, this title helps us to rank higher in search engines. While coding the title tag, you should ensure that your keywords are in title tag. For better search engine results, each page of your website should have unique title containing keywords.

Meta Tags
The main meta tag you should care about is called the "meta description tag". It does not have impact on the search engine ranking, but it tells your visitors about your site. The meta tags have been discussed in the previous chapter. It is always better to use all your keywords in meta tags.
Headings
These are similar to headings in a book, but they have a specific order:  H1, H2, H3, H4, and so on, with H1 as the main heading. The remaining heading codes descend to lower level headings on the page.

# `<h1>Heading</h1>`

## `<h2>Heading</h2>`

### `<h3>Heading</h3>`

#### `<h4>Heading</h4>`

##### `<h5>Heading</h5>`

###### `<h6>Heading</h6>`

```
    <div class="getreport_leftpic"><img src="http:/
    righccone >
    <h1 style="font-size:200%  important; line-heig
    <form method="post" class="af-form-wrapper" act
y: none;">
n" name="meta_web_form_id" value="96676384" />
n" name="meta_split_id" value="" />
n" name="listname" value="backlinkoreport" />
n" name="redirect" value="http://backlinko.com/al

n" name="meta_adtracking" value="Backlinko_Opt-Ir
n" name="meta message" value="1" />
```

For example:
`<h1>How to Optimize Your Website for Search Engines</h1>`
`<h2>The basics of SEO</h2>`
`<h3>SEO Guide</h3>`
You should note the pattern. The more specific your content becomes, the higher the number of the heading becomes.
In general, there should be only one H1 tag on each page, and there can be as many h2s, h3s, and h4s as needed.

Sitemaps

Sitemaps are roadmap for search engines. They give search engines the directions to all of the different pages on your website, ensuring that bots find everything,
There are two types of sitemaps: HTML sitemaps and XML sitemaps. XML sitemaps are coded specifically for search engines, while HTML sitemaps are easy for people to read. You can give link to sitemap, giving the visitor an overview of all pages.
If you have less than a few pages, you should place a link to each page in your HTML sitemap. If your web site has thousands of pages then link only to the most important pages. XML sitemap contain all pages, even if you have millions of pages.

Domain Name

Domain names that have keywords within them rank a lot higher than domains without keywords. If the domain name matches exact keyword, it even rank even higher.
But exact match domains aren't available. That's why many companies use jumbled words for their domain name and build a company around it.

## URL Structure

URLs are another important part of SEO, but it is often overlooked.
If your URLs are clumsy, then search engines will find it difficult while indexing them, and if search engines have a hard time indexing them, then your ranking will suffer.
Remember these factors to keep your URLs more search engine friendly:

- URLs should not contain special characters as $ @ ! * % = ?
- Shorter URL name rank higher.
- Only use letters and numbers.
- Do not use underscore, prefer dashes, as search engines like the
- Sub-domains can rank higher than sub directories.

## Site Structure

The way you link web pages with each other makes an impact on your rankings. Here are some important tips for cross-linking your web site:

- Links within the content have more weight than links within a sidebar or footer.
- keep the number of links on each page under 50.

## Alt Tags

For search engine bots to index images properly, alt tags are needed, adding a brief description. For example, if there is an image of a "pizza", it would tell the search engine that the image is a pizza by using an alt tag. It would look something like this:
<img src="http://igurucool.in/images/pizza.jpg" alt="pizza" />
In addition, ensure your image names are relevant to the image you have put. The picture of the pizza would be called pizza.jpg instead of image1.jpg.

This is the ALT Tag

sizes: 13-inch, 15-inch, and 17-inch.

The MacBook Pro family. High preformance comes in three sizes: 13-inch, 15-inch, and 17-inch.

Only at the Apple Online Store ▶    Hot News Headlines    All    Mac

## Chapter 7: Naming of Pages to Be SEO Friendly and Content Creation

This is the simplest part of the SEO, yet many people do not follow it. It is mandatory to get your website ranked higher in search engine, as well as your individual pages to be ranked higher in the search engines. Suppose your website has page about "cabs for rent in newyork", then the best thing to do is to name your page as: cabs-for-rent-in-newyork.html

You should change the title and the meta-tags of this page accordingly. The number of times the word "cabs for rent in newyork" should appear in the content should be between 4 and 8. Write logical paragraphs and emphasize on this phrase often.

Now if you put the above picture on the page of your website, then the best way would be to give alt tag of this image as "cabs for rent in newyork"

## Chapter 8: The AHREFS Tag

The syntax of a link is as following: <a href="http://www.igurucool.in">The Hot Religion </a>; the site is put inside the parenthesis and the keyword is put outside the brackets.
The best place to build backlinks is the Wordpress blogs and there are billions of them on the internet. They have three fields, and if you want to build links with them, this is the method

Name: Cabs for Rent in Newyork
Email: randy@newyorkcabbie.com
Website: http://www.newyorkcabbie.com

Comment: If you are in Newyork then please visit my website to have a nice ride around New York.

Do this to as many WordPress Blogs, Forums and Posts. The maximum number of times you link your keyword and website, the higher would be the search engine ranking of your website.

So this is the best method to increase your backlinks. The more number of WordPress blogs, where you leave a comment with your keywords and website reference, the higher would be ranking of your website. Now instead of using a long-tail name for the webpage, I use a simple page name called newyorkcab.html, for our website igurucool.in, and now I have to propagate http://www.igurucool.in/newyorkcab.html through-out the internet, just see what I am going to do.

# The Digital Version of this book is available at:

# https://www.amazon.com/dp/B01GT19AV8

**Chapter 9: The easy Places to obtain High Priority Backlinks**

The easy places to obtain high priority backlinks are Twitter, Facebook, Blogger, YouTube, LinkedIn and Google Plus. If you have started a new website and want 6000 backlinks then you can obtain 1000 backlinks each from these sites and it will also increase your social signals.

First with Twitter:
Tweet
#startup http://www.igurucool.in/newyorkcab.html
#crowdfunding http://www.igurucool.in/newyorkcab.html
@billgates http://www.igurucool.in/newyorkcab.html
@shanisadh19 http://www.igurucool.in/newyorkcab.html

Similarly in 40 groups of Facebook post the URL

In 1000 blogs of blogger post the URL

In 1000 videos of YouTube post the URL in the comment field.

In 50 Groups of LinkedIn post the URL 20 times, within a span of one month

Make 20 Videos on YouTube, and share it 1000 times in Google Plus circles making another 1000 links.

If you want any further tips then please write to me at: shivshakti1949(at)outlook(dot)com

### Chapter 10: Link Exchange

There are two great sites through which you can exchange links with thousands of users. These sites are:
- Link2me.com
- Linkmarket.net

You can also search the web for link partners.

### Chapter 11: Keyword Density

Keyword density means number of times the particular keyword should appear in the given page. For 100 words, the ideal occurrence of keyword should be 4 to 6. Do not cramp the webpage with keywords. If you are going to take help of a freelancer then it is advised to use long-tail keywords.

### Crafting Your Main Content

Once you have selected the right keywords, it is important to start crafting your content.

Search engines have bots that automatically crawl and index your website, reading the content to find out what is your site all about and then then the algorithm of search engines decide which keywords of your pages should rank for. You can rank higher for certain keywords depending upon how you frame your content.

But you should not write solely for search engines, this will make content boring for readers. You should write content in such a way that it is search engine friendly and interesting to readers.

You should pay attention to:

- Titles – Create catchy titles that evince interest from readers. You should make a lasting impression on your visitor.
- Keywords – Choose keywords that will attract visitors to your site and are relevant
- Links – Link to quality sites in your niche.
- Freshness – Publish fresh content and maintain its quality.


## Chapter 12: Search Engine Tools and Services

I have outlined the various search engine tools and services, which would be helpful in finding the number of backlinks, building backlinks and other seo related stuff.

- Ahrefs.com –For checking the number of backlinks
- Majestic.com –For checking the number of backlinks
- Dropmylink.com –For building Do Follow Backlink
- XML Sitemap –This is essential part of SEO, this can be generated at: https://www.xml-sitemaps.com/
- Prchecker.info – This can be used to check the page rank of your website.
- You can sign up for Google Analytics and Webmaster Tools from Google Console.
- Given below in red is the robots.txt file in which you only change the name of site and copy-paste it as it is:
  User-Agent: *
  Disallow:
  Allow: /index.html
  Allow: /books.html
  Allow: /contact.html
  Allow: /videos.html
  Allow: /donate.html

  Sitemap: http://www.igurucool.in/sitemap.xml
- Fiverr.com –For Building Bulk Links
- Seoclerk.com –For Building Bulk Links


## Chapter 13: Making Bulk links

I am giving direct links to the services from where you can build bulk links:

- https://www.fiverr.com/uptotop/make-25000-blog-comments-with-scrapebox-get-huge-link-juice
- https://www.fiverr.com/seo_cloud/do-seo-backlinks-pyramid-good-youtube-facebook-quality-edu-high-pr-iinks

- https://www.fiverr.com/spookseo/create-800-social-bookmark-seo-backlinks-ping-in-24-hours
- https://www.fiverr.com/volarex/do-18000-contextual-backlinks-from-6000-wiki-pages-including-real-seo-edu-links
- https://www.fiverr.com/alex_rumer/provide-over-20000-live-seo-blog-comment-backlinks-improve-your-link-building

These services would cost you around $30, but your links would be flooded on the internet. You would shoot to top rankings of all search engines except Google.

## Chapter 14: Making Good links

Building good links or do-follow links is time consuming and tedious process. When I checked last time on flippa, I saw that there were more than 1.7 million sites listed for sale. The web business is down the dumps and 98% of site owners are generating zero revenue. This is because they are not getting any traffic to their site.

Building do-follow links are tedious, but if you want to build them use dropmylink.com, and leave comments as I have mentioned in previous chapter.

Use mostly WordPress blogs to comments. I think that if WordPress is down, then entire SEO business will meet Doom's Day.

## Chapter 15: How to Open Flood Gates of Traffic –Elements of Viral Marketing

The traditional methods of Internet Marketing do not work anymore. It is complete waste of money to advertise on Internet. I have not heard about a single person, who made a penny by advertising on Internet. You can build a brand name on internet by advertising, but money would not come in. There is only one way to open flood gates of traffic that is by viral marketing. Get in touch with any renowned company to execute your viral marketing strategy. Outlined below is the Viral Marketing Strategy.

The first thing which you can do to make your website or project viral is to create 20 Power Point slides about your product and website and upload it on www.slideshare.com so that while you are working on other aspects of your projects, there is general awareness about your product.

Now getting into the concept of viral marketing, let me tell you how viral marketing works. In viral marketing one person says another person, another person says third person; the third person says to a bunch of people and this carries on. Thus the word of mouth spreads and people start talking about your product or website.

Some people sign up for your products and services and you convince them to spread the word about your products and services by giving an incentive or feel good factor.

Now coming to the execution part of viral marketing; the first thing which you have to do is to make a website. The process of creating the website is mentioned in:

- The complete guide to Internet Marketing for starters and beginners
  Link: http://www.amazon.com/gp/product/B013DZC452

Building a website is very simple. You can download the template from the website css3templates.co.uk; then you can use coffee cup html to edit the files and upload it on the server. If you want interactivity in the website then you can use PHP in your website. You can get PHP developers from odesk.com, guru.com or elance.com. Do not use any other site for building your PHP website because other websites like freelancer.com are scam sites. They will steal your money from your credit card, debit card or PayPal account. You can use freelancer.com with your debit card only if you have small amount of money in your bank account.

Once you have created your account in odesk.com, elance.com or guru.com then follow the steps further mentioned. I would recommend you to have a Gmail account for all purposes because Gmail is the most powerful mail and it has the most advanced features. The second most powerful mail is outlook.com. The emails like yahoo are good but its anti-spam features makes you difficult to deal with bulk mail which you would require in the later stage. It would be good if you create an outlook mail as well because it will help you to create Skype account which would be handy for you to deal with project developers.

Once you have created your account in jobsites, you create a Skype account using the outlook mail service. Skype would be handy for you for conversing with freelancers and clients; obviously you can check details through email. Attaching PayPal account with the jobsites is important because it adds credibility to your account.

You should post projects under the following heads:

- PHP/Website Design
- Logo Design
- SEO
- Shopping Cart

It would be good if you post all four projects in all three sites: odesk.com, guru.com and elance.com

The posting of projects solve two purposes: It creates awareness about your product or website and secondly you get important projects done.

Host your website only at net4.in, as other hosts have tendency to upsell and provide bad services. Never host your website at bigrock.in; it is the biggest fraud on Internet.

The social media plays an important role in Internet Marketing. The major social media channels are: Twitter, YouTube, Facebook, LinkedIn and Google Plus. You have to use them at fullest extent to generate leads and sales and to make your website viral. The best website for displaying and sharing video about your product or service is YouTube. If you ask how to make a video then it is pretty simple.

Make a Power Point Presentation in Microsoft Office and put information about your product and services in between of something informative. To see how product related video should be visit www.igurucool.in. Once you are done with Power Point Presentation, save the file and upload it to slideshare.net. After that in Power Point go to File > Save and Send > Videos > HD and Internet and save the video as .wmv file. The Power Point does it automatically. Set the spacing between each slides as 11 seconds in the video. If you put shorter duration then the viewers would not be able to comprehend the message conveyed in the video. After you upload your Video on YouTube – Make sure that you put keyword rich title, description and tags. Your video can be discovered by viewers only through the keyword –On Google or on YouTube.

Keep sharing your video through Twitter, LinkedIn, Posting video link in the comment section of YouTube, Facebook and Google Plus. More you share the video, more people will view the video and more people will come to know about your product and services. Never put a link in the description section of the YouTube or you would be banned from the YouTube, but it is ok to put your links in the comment section of other people videos. Once the video is published, be sure to review it and like it.

The best way of viral marketing is to keep on posting comments in the YouTube videos of other people. I just posted the following comment in the videos and within minutes I had 107 hits to my website.

One World, One Religion, No Discrimination:

http://www.amazon.com/gp/product/B01BION45O

www.igurucool.in

www.kalkie.in

www.kalkie.org

www.cidf.in

You should write twenty eBooks about your product for length of thirty to forty pages and publish it online to increase the awareness about your website or product. Once people read your eBooks and if they find something interesting they would definitely visit your website to find something more about your product. Use Foxy Form to contact the visitors from your website, because if you give them your direct email they will spam you.

Collect data about your potential customers in an excel sheet and regular keep sending newsletters to them. The eBook is best written in Microsoft word and you do not have to go to any online editor as Microsoft Word itself checks for spelling mistakes and grammar. You can use freepdfconvert.com to convert your book into PDF format and distribute it through emails to your friends and associates. Do not forget to insert links about your websites in that book. Writing books can be additional source of income to you.

You can use voiceover artists at odesk.com to convert your eBooks into audio format or record the speech of text yourself. You can upload the audio into Apple iTunes to increase the awareness about your product and increase virility.

Banner advertisement is one of the best ways to attract traffic to your website and increase awareness about your product. There are some sites which are free; you get tons of traffic from them –and there are some sites where you have to pay a small amount for attracting the traffic, but nevertheless the returns are good. If someone does not click on your banner, then also he or she learns about your product and a lasting impression is left on mind.

The first thing which you have to do is to create a 468x60 pixel banner at the site www.bannerfans.com. Use only two lines of text to create the banner; more lines in the text would distract the visitor, and your message is not left to him. In the first line of text mention about your product, in the second line of text add the URL of the site or landing page.

Now upload the banner in the way that you can remember the purpose for which you have created it. Suppose you have created a banner about the stuff you are selling on your website, then after downloading the banner from bannerfans.com, rename it as bannerbook.jpg; and then upload it on the server of your website. Be sure to place it in the root directory. You would need to upload it or link it with various websites which do banner exchange. The prominent sites for banner exchange are:

- Easyhits4u.com
- Hit4hit.org
- Bannerexchang.com

You can also run the pay-per-click advertisement in Google Adwords. The cost of campaign is less, the visibility is more. New people will come to know about your website. If the link to banner leads to a giveaway then there would be swarm of traffic to your website.

To make your banner campaign viral, it is recommended that you use AddThis to your webpage or landing page in such a way that people are compelled to share your webpage with others through Facebook, Twitter, LinkedIn or email.

Another example of automatic traffic exchange is www.hitleap.com. You can create a hitleap account; add up to three websites in the hitleap traffic exchange for views up to 20 seconds. Then you can download the hitleap viewer and install it on your computer to run the automatic traffic exchange. When the traffic exchange starts working then you start viewing other people websites and they in return view your website.

There can be flood gates of traffic opening to your website through Twitter. Use a Marketing Tweet and get it automatically retweeted by following sites:

- Traffup.net
- Like4like.org
- Followlike.net

## Chapter 16: 100K Hits to brand new website within an hour

Well if you have ten computers located at ten different locations and ten people with you and $100 to spare then I will give you a simple method to generate 100K hits within an hour. The method is like nuclear fission. I will tell nuclear fusion in a later book –in which 10 Million hits are generated to a brand new website within an hour. So here are the steps:

- Tell all ten people to install hitleap.com viewer and at all three slots of hitleap, load three webpages of your website.
- Pay $40 to neobux.com and $40 to clixsense.com and schedule the ad at 8 PM sharp
- Pay $20 to Adf.ly and schedule the US hits at 8 PM sharp

- Make 10 Gmail accounts, and open 10 YouTube Channel from each account

Then exactly at 7:50 PM start firing:

- Open the hitleap viewer at all ten locations
- Make an ad about your website and paste it in the comment field of YouTube videos for next 45 minutes.
- By that time neobux.com, clixsense.com and adf.ly had started firing.

The last time I tried this on client, his website had 218,986 hits in a span of one hour.

*Now to rank higher, again work on these areas:*

- Domain Authority –The content in Wikipedia, LinkedIn and other top sites will have high ranking.
- Freshness of Content
- Number of do-follow backlinks
- Number of no-follow backlinks
- Social Signals from content posted in YouTube, Facebook, LinkedIn, SlideShare, Twitter etc.
- Keyword Density –The ideal keyword density in content should be 5-10%
- Meta Tags –So that Search Engines can crawl the keywords in Meta Tags.
- Relevance of Content
- No of Mentions in Social Media, Groups and Forums
- Page Rank – That is the quality of Backlinks
- Mobile Friendliness of Site –If your site is mobile friendly, ranking is higher.
- Age of the Site –Older the site, higher would be its ranking
- Popularity of the Site – Depending upon the Alexa Rank of Site, the keywords are ranked. (Suppose there are 1 million hits to your website within hour, and then all keywords would rank in top 10).
- Speed of the Site –The lesser time the site takes to load –higher it would be ranked.
- Security of the site –(https:// sites are ranked higher)

## Chapter 17: Handy Tips and Tricks

While you are building links, use Ahrefs.com to track your links –the screen shot from Ahrefs.com would look like following:

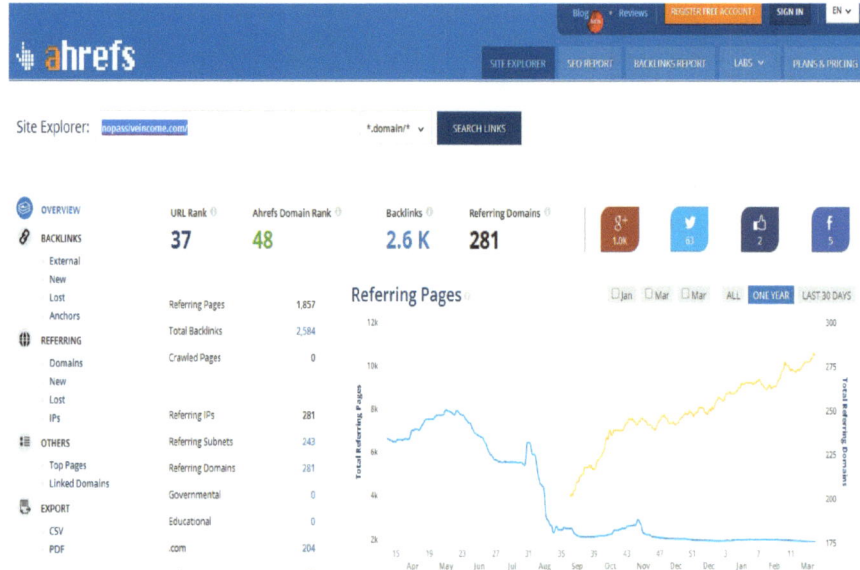

Here you get information about the following things:

- Total Number of Back Links
- Total Number of Referring Domains
- Total Number of EDU and Gov Links
- Social Signals

The importance of Edu and Gov Links is that it carries 20 times link juice more than a normal Do-follow Backlink. And as I mentioned earlier –more the number of referring domains to your website –higher will be the ranking of Website. So if you go for Bulk links, immediately 2500+ domains will start pointing towards your website.

Another handy tool to analyze your backlinks is majestic.com; here are few screen shots from the site:

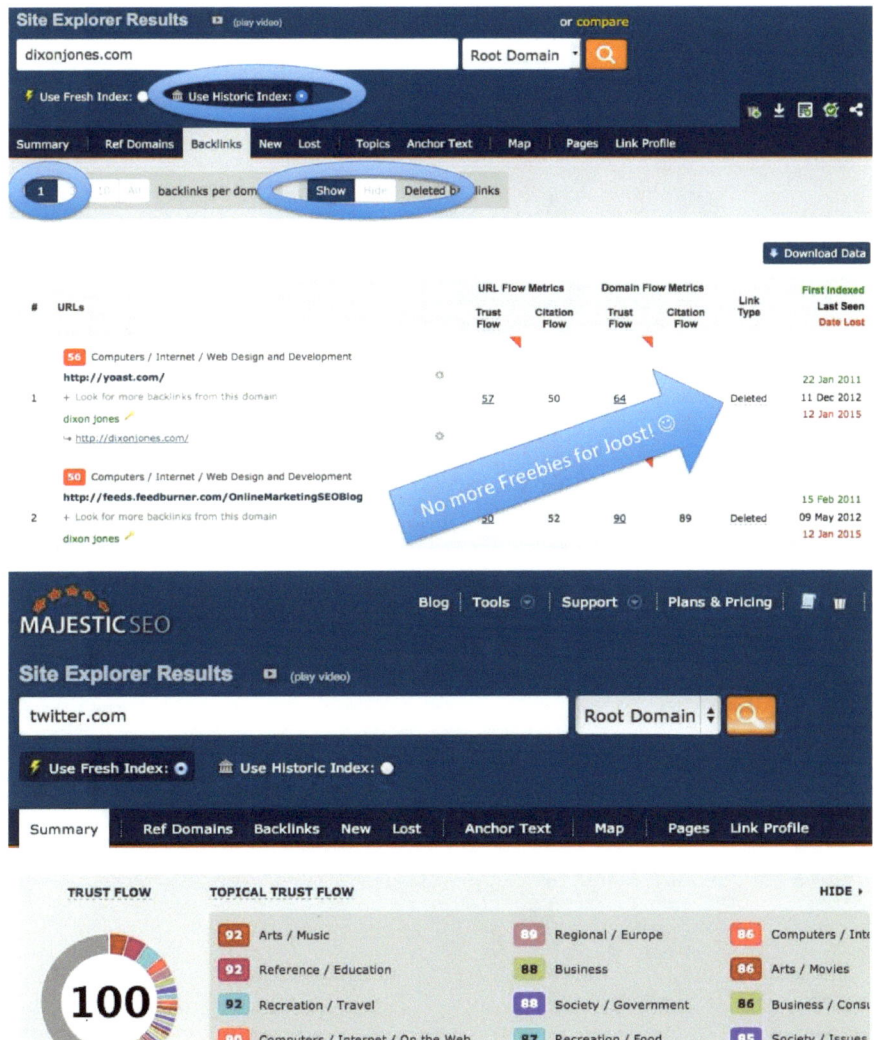

## Count of TopicalTrustFlow_Topic_1

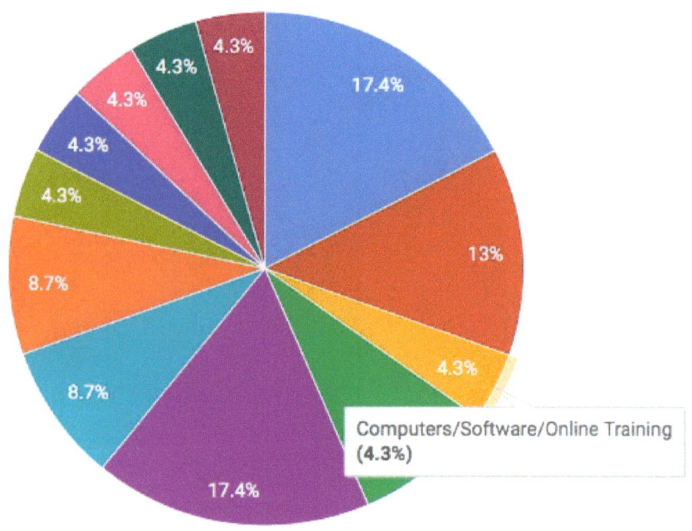

Now you would be able to find most of the edu or gov blogs with the help of Dropmylink.com, but in case you are unable to find, here is the strategy: In order to find edu and gov blogs, we have to use specific Google searches that give us .Edu or .Gov results for keywords we search. Paste the following searches into Google and put your main keyword into the "keyword" section of the code:

site:.edu inurl:blog "comment" -"you must be logged in" -"posting closed" -"comment closed" "keyword"

site:.edu "no comments" +blogroll -"posting closed" -"you must be logged in" -"comments are closed"

site:.gov "no comments" +blogroll -"posting closed" -"you must be logged in" -"comments are closed"

inurl:(edu|gov) "no comments" +blogroll -"posting closed" -"you must be logged in" -"comments are closed"

site:.edu inurl:wp-login.php +blog

site:.gov inurl:wp-login.php +blog

site:.edu inurl:"wp-admin" +login

By using these searches, you can locate blogs with .Edu or .Gov extensions, allowing you to gain extra link juice for your links.

Now to sum up this book, here are the top 21 things -which you have to keep in mind while doing SEO:

1. Commit yourself to the optimization. SEO is not a one-time event. SEO requires a long-term mindset and commitment from your side.


2. Have faith in your ability and remain patient. It takes months before actual results start pouring in.

3. If you are hiring a SEO company then ask questions about the tactics they are adopting to rank your site and time frame.

4. Learn SEO all by yourself. It is an art. More you practice, more perfect you will become.

5. Have analytics like ahrefs.com, majestic.com, statcounter.com and Google Analytics to measure your efforts.

6. Follow the rules of SEO to build an attractive website with sitemap and robots.txt in place.

7. Include a site map page. Spiders can't index pages that can't be crawled.

8. Make the navigation of your site simple.

9. Do keyword research at the start of web business? Use the free versions of Keyword Discovery or Word Tracker. Another good free tool is Google's Ad Words Keyword Tool.

10. Run a PPC campaign either in Google's Ad Words or Facebook, and measure results. This will keep you happy till SEO starts showing results.

11. Write a unique and relevant title and Meta description on every page.

12. Write for your users, not for the search engines. It's the users who buy, not search engines

13. Write great and unique content; keep it refreshing every now and then.

14. Use your keywords as anchor text when you are linking your webpages internally.

15. Do directory submission at trusted sources. One of the trusted sources for directory submission is Directory Maximizer (http://www.directorymaximizer.com). Do Dmoz and Yahoo submission as well.

16. Distribute Press Release wisely to gain media attention and create a niche for yourself.

17. Start a blog on Wordpress and link it to your site. Participate with other related blogs. Search engines, Google especially, love blogs for fresh content.

18. Use social media marketing to leverage your website. Make Facebook Fan-Page, Make Twitter account and link both buttons on front page of your website. Generate content for Quora and Yahoo answers, linking back to your website. Make more than 50K connections on LinkedIn and Post Regularly leaving links back to your website. You can use Flickr, Tumblr and Stumble Upon to redirect hoards of traffic to your website.

19. Make vantage point for local search opportunities. Ensure your site is listed in local/social directories such as CitySearch, Yelp, Local.com, etc., and encourage your visitors and customers to leave good reviews of your business on these sites, too.


20. Sign up for Google Webmaster Central, Bing Webmaster Tools and Yahoo Site Explorer to analyze how many numbers of links to your website are counted,

21. Have multiple traffic sources to your website. The ideal source of traffic should be mix of search, ppc, facebook groups, twitter followers, youtube videos, newsletter, direct traffic, reddit, stumble upon, links left at forums and other social media.

## The Digital Version of this book is available at:

## https://www.amazon.com/dp/B01GT19AV8

# End of Book